BOBSLEDDING AND THE LUGE

A TRUE BOOK

by

Larry Dane Brimner

Children's Press®
A Division of Grolier Publishing
New York London Hong Kong Sydney
Danbury, Connecticut

Reading Consultant
Linda Cornwell
Learning Resource Consultant
Indiana Department
of Education

Author's Dedication
For Sneed B. Collard III

A bobsled team pushes
their sled at the
beginning of the race.

Library of Congress Cataloging-in-Publication Data

Brimner, Larry Dane.
    Bobsledding and the luge / by Larry Dane Brimner.
        p.   cm. — (A true book)
    Includes bibliographical references (p.) and index.
    Summary: Describes the history of bobsledding and luge competi-
tion, with a look at these sports at the Olympics.
    ISBN 0-516-20436-X (lib. bdg.)   0-516-26203-3 (pbk.)
    1. Bobsledding—Juvenile literature. [1. Bobsledding. 2. Olympics.]
I. Title. II. Series.
GV856.B75 1997   97-2271
796.9'5—dc21   CIP
                                                              AC

Contents

A bobsled speeds through a turn.

Down the Chute!

A bobsled rockets down the icy chute. The driver and crew are tucked low to help increase their speed. They lean, preparing to round a curve. As they do, the bobsled climbs the frozen walls of the chute. For a moment, it seems as if the bobsled might leave the chute completely and launch into space. It doesn't! Instead, the bobsled explodes out of the curve. It speeds down the chute toward the finish line. Will the crew win the race?

Bobsled racing began in the winter of 1888–89 when an Englishman had an idea. He was in Switzerland and noticed that sleds were used to haul wood over the snow and ice.

In the past, sleds were necessary to gather wood during the winter.

Wood-hauling sleds were practical tools in snowy Switzerland. They were also simple in design. Two wooden runners slid over the frozen surface. Wood for winter fires was piled on animal skins that stretched between the runners. The Englishman wondered if a sled could also be used for racing.

He tied two of the sleds together. For a brake, he attached a rake that he could drag in the snow. Then he took off down a slope. It was a success! And the activity quickly caught on with wealthy people.

They formed racing clubs and held contests. The original races were held on icy roads

One of the first
bobsled runs

and mountain passes, but people wanted greater speed. To achieve this, racers would lean back and jerk forward. This "bobbing" motion gave the sport its name.

Still, racers wanted to go even faster, so they built special raceways, called "bobruns." They were coated with ice and had steep sides. The steep sides kept the bobsled on the run, which allowed it to go faster. In the winter of 1889–90,

the first steel sled was intro-
duced. It went faster still.
Since then, people have con-
tinued to work on new
designs, which use stronger,
lightweight materials to
increase the sled's speed.

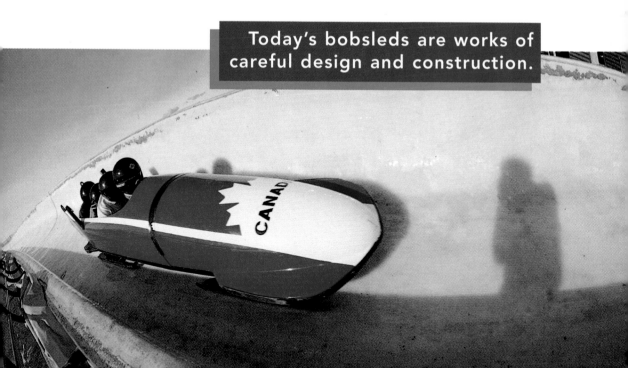

Today's bobsleds are works of careful design and construction.

Bobsledding Today

Bobsledding has been part of the Olympics since the first Winter Games in 1924. The only time the event did not take place was in 1960, when weather and time kept a bobsled run from being built. Today's bobsleds, however, do not look like those used at the first Olympic Winter Games.

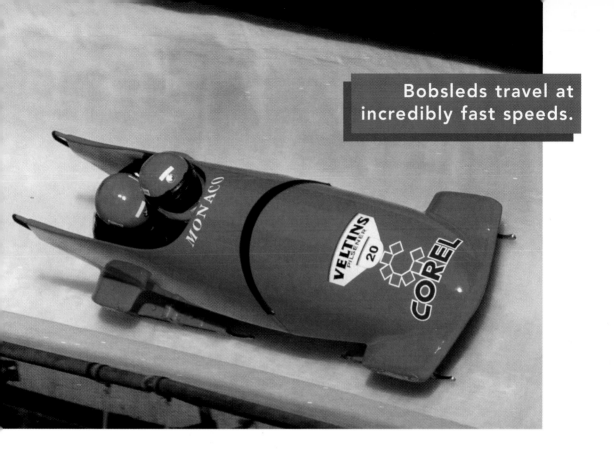

Bobsleds travel at incredibly fast speeds.

Today's sleds are built of fiberglass and steel. Looking more like missiles than wood-hauling sleds, they skim over ice at lightning-fast speeds. Without goggles, it would be impossible for racers to see.

A two-man bobsled (top) and a four-man bobsled (bottom)

Bobsleds come in two sizes, one for two-man teams and the other for four-man teams. (Women do not yet compete at the Olympic level in bobsledding.) A two-man sled cannot weigh more than 390 kilograms (859 pounds), including the riders.

A four-man sled is limited to 630 kilograms (1,389 pounds). Weight and gravity carry the sled and riders down the bobrun.

Bobruns have also changed. Today's courses twist and turn. They are concrete chutes that are refrigerated for the best possible ice conditions.

Beneath the bobrun ice is a base of concrete.

One of the most important parts of a race is the start. Racers run and push the sled into the chute. To keep from slipping, they wear cleated shoes that grip the ice. They must work as a team to push the sled as fast as possible. Their timing must be perfect.

Gaining speed, they leap into the bobsled right at the starting line. The man in front steers. The man at the rear operates the brake. Only the

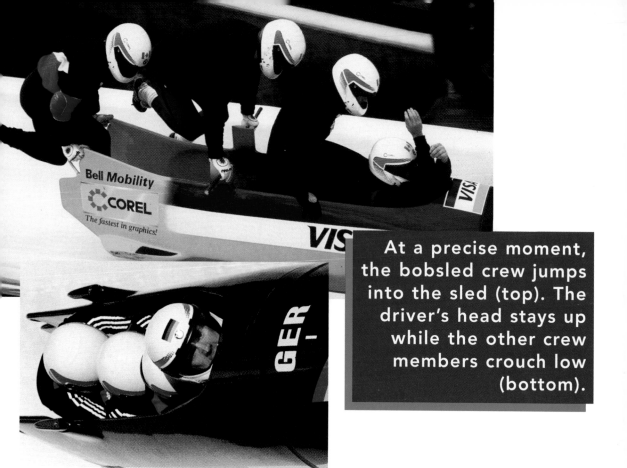

At a precise moment, the bobsled crew jumps into the sled (top). The driver's head stays up while the other crew members crouch low (bottom).

driver keeps his head up. The others tuck themselves low so they will go as fast as they possibly can. (Racers no longer bob their upper bodies.)

The bobsled explodes down the run, hitting speeds of 100 miles (161 kilometers) per hour and greater. One error could spell disaster. At this speed, a crash could result in injury—or death. From start to finish, a record-breaking race lasts less than a minute. And each run is a dangerous new adventure.

This bobsled crashed and turned over after taking a turn too quickly.

Olympic Sportsmanship

A shining example of the Olympic Creed was the Italian bobsledder Eugenio Monti. He was known to be a fierce competitor. But he was also a fair-minded sportsman.

Monti had fought unsuccessfully for twelve years to win a gold medal in the two-man bobsled event. At the 1964 Games in Innsbruck, Austria, he was once again in the running for a gold medal.

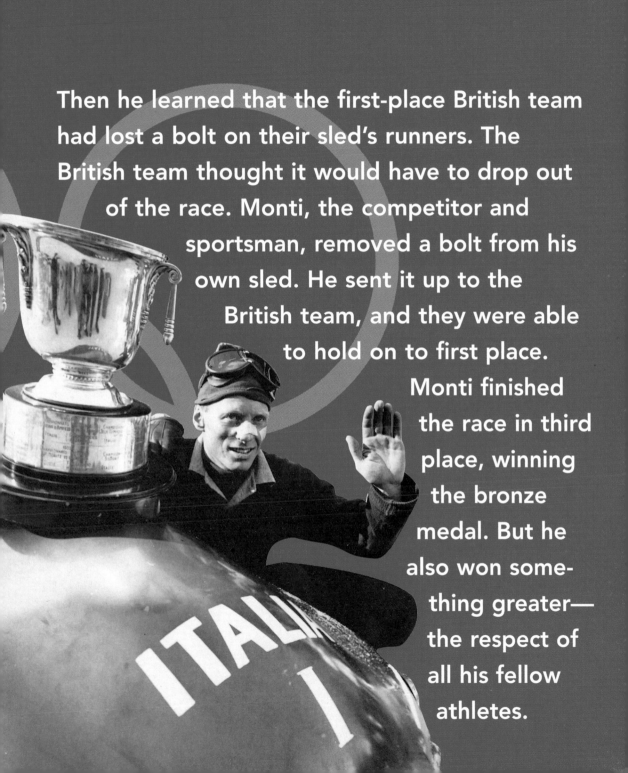

Then he learned that the first-place British team had lost a bolt on their sled's runners. The British team thought it would have to drop out of the race. Monti, the competitor and sportsman, removed a bolt from his own sled. He sent it up to the British team, and they were able to hold on to first place. Monti finished the race in third place, winning the bronze medal. But he also won something greater— the respect of all his fellow athletes.

The Luge

Like bobsledders, luge racers shoot down steep, ice-covered tracks. Both men and women compete in this sport, though in separate events. Men compete against each other in one- and two-person events. Women compete only in one-person events.

Luge takes place on a track
similar to a bobsled run.

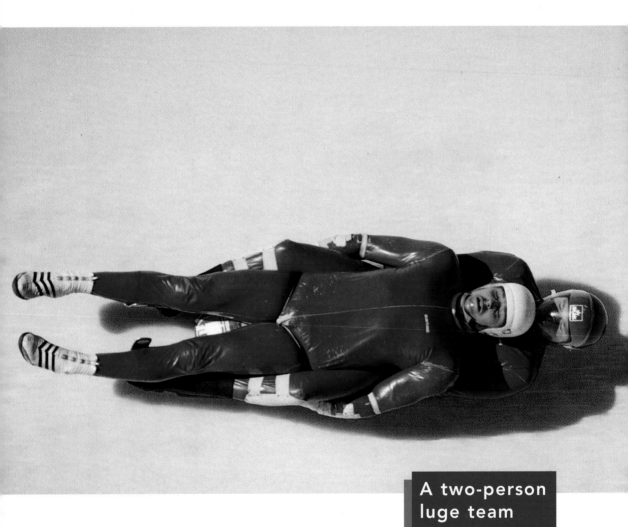

A two-person
luge team

Luge sleds are similar to toboggans, and the racers are called "sliders."

Luge is one of the most dangerous sports in the Olympics. Lying on their backs, sliders rocket down runs feet first. They steer their sleds with gentle leg and shoulder pressure. To increase their speed, sliders wear suits, helmets, and special pointed booties. A practiced slider reaches speeds up to

80 miles (128 kilometers) per hour.

To start a race, sliders rock back and forth on their sleds. Then they push off with force. They wear spiked gloves and use their hands to catch the ice and thrust themselves forward. This helps to increase their speed. Then gravity takes over, and it's a downhill race against the clock to the end of the run.

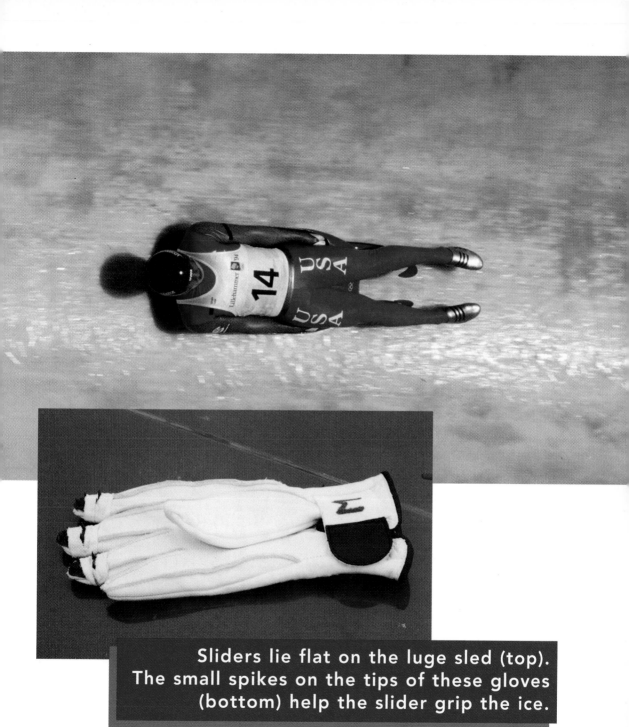

Sliders lie flat on the luge sled (top).
The small spikes on the tips of these gloves
(bottom) help the slider grip the ice.

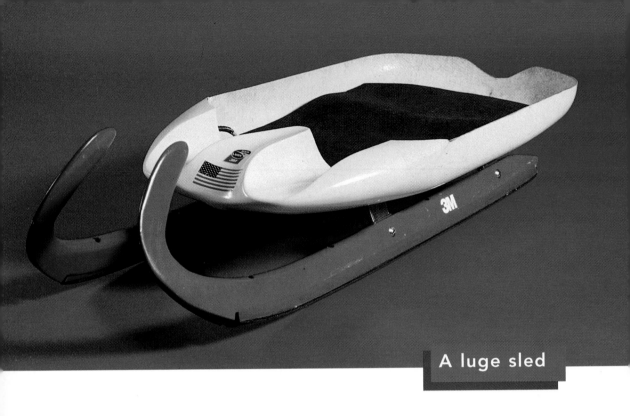

A luge sled

Luge sleds are speed machines. Wood, fiberglass, or plastic runners support hardened steel blades. To make the sled even faster, sliders polish and sharpen the blades again and again.

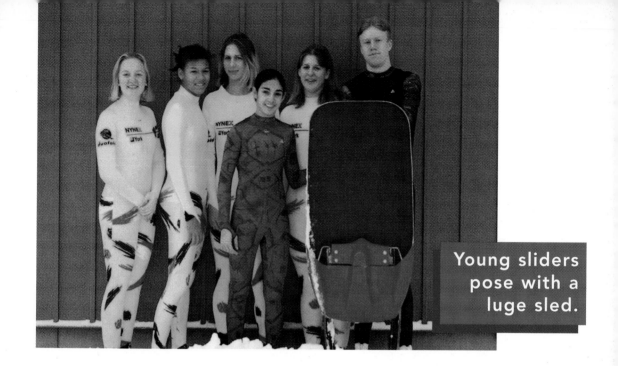

Young sliders
pose with a
luge sled.

Although luge competition
dates back to 1883, it has been
part of the Winter Olympic
Games only since 1964. All
seventy-two Olympic luge
medals have been won by four
countries—Germany, Austria,
Italy, and the U.S.S.R. (Russia).

What a Run!

Bobsled and luge runs are extremely difficult to build and maintain. There are only a small number of them in the world today. Each one offers different kinds of excitement and challenges to sliders. Some are short and full of twists. Others are straight and steep. Here are four different luge runs from around the world:

Start

Nagano, Japan

Start

**Lake Placid,
USA**

Finish

	Length	Curves
Men	930m	14
Women	740m	11

Finish

	Length	Curves
Men	1326m	14
Women	1194m	13

Start

Start

**Königsee,
Germany**

**Calgary,
Canada**

Finish

Finish

	Length	Curves
Men	1300m	16
Women	1225m	12

	Length	Curves
Men	1251m	14
Women	1185m	10

A New Twist

People are always inventing new ways to play old sports. A new twist to luge is street luge. Street luge has been around since the early 1980s. It's a blend of ice luge and skateboarding.

Street luge uses a stretched-out skateboard that is usually

Street luge takes place on road surfaces, not ice.

built of a light metal called aluminum. A slider, or pilot, rides it the same way one rides an ice luge—with no

Several sets of wheels allow the sled to move down a run.

seat belt or brakes. Instead of rocketing down an icy chute, however, a street luge pilot zooms along just inches above asphalt.

Like luge, street luge is a high-speed, high-risk sport. Pilots must wear special gear to protect themselves against injury. A leather suit is specially fitted to each slider. Ultra-padded gloves are needed. Many street lugers also wear motorcycle helmets.

Street luge is not yet part of the Olympics. Still, street luge racers do compete against each other. The International Luge Road Racing Association

organizes many events. Also, street luge and other unusual, high-speed sports are featured every year at the Extreme Games. They are called the "Extreme Games" because of the dangerous nature of the sports.

Olympic Moments

The Olympic Winter Games have always been a celebration of the athletes of winter. Naturally, sliders wanted to be a part of it. When they asked that their sport be made a part of the Winter Games, however, critics argued that luge was too

It is always a scary moment when a slider loses control of the sled.

dangerous. In 1964, sliders were finally given a chance. Unfortunately, luge in the Olympics got off to a sad beginning. Two weeks before the 1964 Games were to open, there was a serious accident. Kazimierz Kay-Skrzypeski, a Polish-born British slider, was killed on a trial run of the Olympic course.

The Olympics are a stage for triumph as well as tragedy. In 1928, Billy Fiske was chosen to drive the four-man bobsled for the United States. He was only sixteen years old. By leading the team to victory, he became the youngest man

ever to win a gold medal at the Winter Olympics. That record has since been broken by Scott Allen, a fourteen-year-old figure skater. Still, Billy's victory was a big achievement for one so young.

Bobsledding and the luge
are two of the fastest sports
at the Olympics. Participants
are like human missiles on a

The winning U.S. bobsled
team poses in their sled with
other runner-up teams.

Bobsledding (top) and luge (bottom) are two of the fastest sports in the Winter Olympics.

wild roller-coaster ride. In each sport, the goal is to flash to the bottom of the run in record time. Yet the racers are never happy at the bottom of a run. There is always a new record to break, a new run to conquer, and a new competitor to challenge. So they return to the top again and again for another wild ride down the chute.

To Find Out More

Here are some additional resources to help you learn more about bobsledding and the luge:

 **Books**

 **Organizations**

Duden, Jane. **The Olympics.** Macmillan Child Group, 1991.

Greenspan, Bud. **100 Greatest Moments in Olympic History.** General Publishing Group, 1995.

Harris, Jack C. **The Winter Olympics.** Creative Education, Inc., 1990.

Malley, Stephen. **A Kid's Guide to the Nineteen Ninety-Four Winter Olympics.** Bantam Press, 1994.

Wallechinsky, David. **The Complete Book of the Winter Olympics.** Little, Brown & Co., 1993.

U.S. Bobsled and Skeleton Federation (UBSF)
Box 828
Lake Placid, NY 12946

United States Luge Association (USLA)
PO Box 651
35 Church Street
Lake Placid, NY 12946

Internet Sites

2002 Winter Olympic Games Home Page
www.SLC2002.org

A growing web page that provides information on the 2002 Winter Olympics in Salt Lake City.

International Federation of Bobsledding and Tobogganing
www.fibt.corel.com

A list of events and new developments in bobsledding from around the world.

Official 1998 Olympic Web Site
www.nagano.olympic.org

A great source of information on the events of the 1998 Winter Olympics.

Original Luge Home Page
www.luge.com

Learn about the different equipment and techniques necessary to ride the luge.

Skateluge Home Page
www.skateluge.com

Information about skateluge equipment and how to start sliding.

Winter Sports Page
http://www.wintersports.org

A central site to explore winter sports and links to other sites.

Important Words

aluminum light metal used in the construction of bobsleds and luges

blade the part of the bobsled that runs on the ice

bobrun a course designed for a bobsled race

bootie race shoes specially designed for sliders

chute a track with high sides that is specially designed and built for a bobsled

fiberglass a light and strong material used to build bobsleds and luges

runner the part of the bobsled that holds the blades

slider someone who rides on the luge

Index

Meet the Author

Larry Dane Brimner is the author of several books for Children's Press, including five True Books on the Winter Olympics. He is a member of the Authors Guild and the Society of Children's Book Writers and Illustrators. Mr. Brimner makes his home in Southern California and the Rocky Mountains.